THE KIDS' DOG BOOK

Owl Books are published by Greey de Pencier Books, 179 John Street, Suite 500, Toronto, ON M5T 3G5

The Owl colophon is a trademark of Owl Children's Trust Inc. Greey de Pencier Books is a licensed user of trademarks of Owl Children's Trust Inc.

Distributed in the U. S. by Firefly Books (U.S.) Inc., 230 Fifth Ave., Suite 1607, New York, NY 10001

This book was published with the generous support of the Canada Council and the Ontario Arts Council.

Special thanks to Dr. Gary Landsberg for his extensive assistance on the revised edition.

Cataloguing in Publication Data
Main Entry under title:
The Kids dog book

Rev. ed.
ISBN 0-920775-50-0

1. Dogs – juvenile literature.
I. Dingwall, Laima, 1953–   .
II. Slaight, Annabel, 1940–   .

SF426.5.K52 1990   599.74'442   C90-090064-4

Cover Design: Wycliffe Smith, Gary Beelik
Cover Photo: T Grill/Miller Comstock Inc.
Text Design: Nick Milton

Printed in Hong Kong

THE KIDS' DOG BOOK

From the Editors of OWL Magazine

CONTENTS

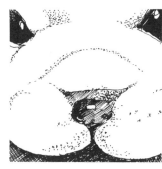

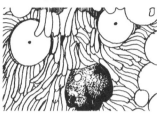

BEST FRIENDS

This book has been created by popular demand. We, the editors of OWL, the Discovery Magazine for Children, have had more requests for information about dogs over the years than almost any other animal. So we decided to make this book for you. We have answered hundreds of your questions by asking top scientists, trainers and veterinarians. We are grateful to them for helping us bring you a book full of the best and latest advice about pets and pet care.

One of the things many kids have asked us is why their dogs behave the way they do. The answer is that pet dogs have the same instincts as their wild relatives. So this book introduces you to many of your dog's canine cousins, too. Forty-four million homes in North America have a dog in the family. So if you're a dog lover, you're in good company. Why are dogs so popular? Everyone seems to have slightly different reasons for loving a dog, so we begin this book with a few real kids praising their best friends. If you were writing about why your dog is important to you what would *you* say?

Laima Dingwall

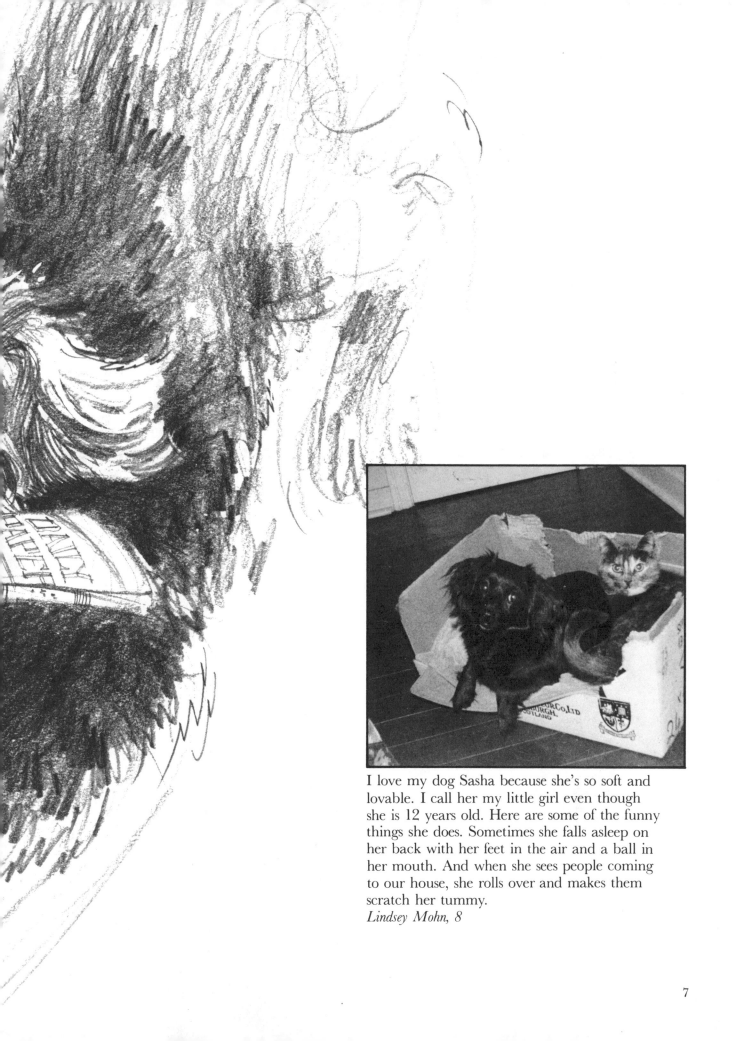

I love my dog Sasha because she's so soft and lovable. I call her my little girl even though she is 12 years old. Here are some of the funny things she does. Sometimes she falls asleep on her back with her feet in the air and a ball in her mouth. And when she sees people coming to our house, she rolls over and makes them scratch her tummy.
Lindsey Mohn, 8

My dog Sara is great because she helps me on my paper route by pulling a toboggan. She was born in Inuvik 12 years ago.
Paul Watson, 10

I love dogs, but me and my Mom are allergic to them. So since I couldn't have a real dog, I decided imaginary ones were just as good. I named my dog Doris after my favorite movie star's show name. She is a Husky. Here she is.
Kristen Butler, 9

I have three dogs and I love them all because they have fluffy fur and they are so adorable. Our smallest dog is called Sparky, our middle-sized dog is called Whiskers, and our big dog is called Sheba, and they are all mutts. *Sarah Lightfoot, 8*

My Poodle Tara is a special friend. She is cute and cuddly, does a variety of tricks and is a good protector.
Lori Rachelle Reker, 11

My dog, named Pebbles, is my part-time pet. I love her because she is very playful. Pebbles loves car rides.
Lisa Sutton, 10

I love my Cocker Spaniel Dusky because she is soft, small, black, playful, furry, gentle and kind, and she loves to play. She's the best (in my opinion).
Kathryn Brimecombe, 10

My dog Ginger is special to me because I can talk to her when I am mad at someone and she won't tell them. I can also watch TV with her. She can do six tricks including balancing a peanut on her nose. *Rhonda Barkey, 12*

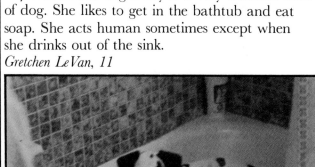

I love my dog Cedar because she is friendly, playful, gentle, protective, caring, funny and she's usually obedient.
Caroline Yeo

My Dalmatian dog Daisy is a very different kind of dog. She likes to get in the bathtub and eat soap. She acts human sometimes except when she drinks out of the sink.
Gretchen LeVan, 11

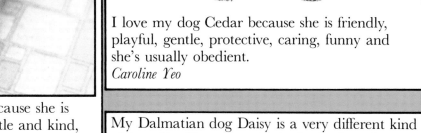

I love my dog very much because she is so faithful. She comes when I call her, protects me and never runs away.
Shannon Corrigan, 10

OUR NEW DOG

from a diary
by Melanie (11) and Marissa (7).

At last our new puppies are born. We are going to find other homes for the males and will keep the female. We've named her Dynamite.

Dynamite is an English Cocker Spaniel. She was born black and white, but has a few spots and patches which will develop into the markings that characterize her breed as she gets older. Some Cockers have red, liver, or brown patches, not just black and white.

WEEK 1
Dynamite and her brothers were born with their eyes closed, and although their ears were formed internally, they were not well enough developed to hear sounds. Food, love and warmth are very important for puppies. From birth until nearly three weeks, the pups depend completely on their mother for food and love. We handle the pups just a few moments a day to help them get used to people.

WEEK 3

Dynamite is certainly proving to be like her name and being just as playful as she can find the energy for. In fact, all the puppies are taking an interest in their surroundings, such as where their bed is, and more so in each other. I think they find it quite funny to discover that there are more little creatures like themselves.

WEEK 6 and 7

Dynamite and her brothers are now completely weaned and no longer need their mother for any nourishment. Now they get four little meals a day. We have been careful not to overfeed them as they have small stomachs and puppies are very greedy!

WEEK 4

They are enjoying playing with one another and it is fun as well as fascinating to watch them observe one another especially as they are starting to bark and growl.

WEEK 8 and 9

Dynamite's brothers have left for new homes. Now that Dynamite is all by herself, house training is our lesson for the week. It is not easy as she does not like going out of the warm house. But as she is taken outside regularly, she will get used to the idea. We are also putting down clean newspaper for her in one part of the house, so that she can use that when she has to.

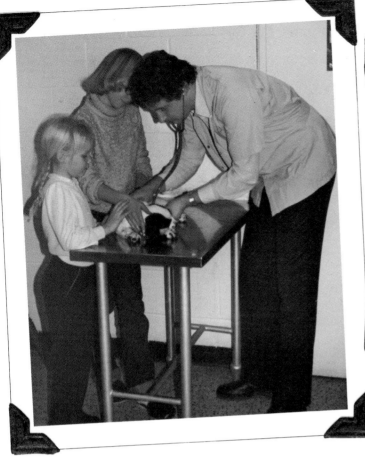

At the end of the eighth week Dynamite went to the veterinarian for her first checkup and immunization shots. The vet checked her heart and lungs, listening with his stethoscope, and felt other parts of her body to make sure everything was all right.

Brushing and grooming a dog is very important, especially to keep its fur in good condition. We decided now was the time for Dynamite to have her first grooming lesson. We put Dynamite on the kitchen table and held and stroked her while we brushed her.

We think she looks very proud sitting in her own new bed, and she also enjoys lying in the bed playing with her chewy toys.

PUPPIES: TO KNOW THEM IS TO LOVE THEM

It's hard to believe that cuddly little Bulldog pups often grow up to look tough and to wear "spiked" collars.

These pups are Springer Spaniels. Hunters bred their ancestors to "spring" at birds.

Can you believe that these three sad-faced Spaniels come from a family of dogs bred to hunt birds called woodcocks? It's true. Hence the name Cocker Spaniel.

The ancient Chinese bred Pekingese to look as lion-like as possible. They found it easier to have dogs around the house than the real thing.

These little Dachshunds will never grow much bigger. They're miniatures and have earned the odd name of mini-wires because of their rough hair.

Who me, a hunter? While all terriers were bred to chase and kill, as pets they're friendly, inquisitive and full of fun.

Do your ears hang low? It doesn't seem to bother these frisky Basset Hound pups.

Shang and Poppy —
Bu Dynasty Chow Chow

If you see dogs with blue-black tongues you can be sure they're Chow Chows. Poppy the puppy and her dad Shang have kindly put on a show for you.

POP DOGS

Is there a Fido in your future? If you have the time, patience and energy to care for a dog, then that's an easy question to answer. But it's not so easy to choose what kind of dog your Fido should be. Believe it or not, there are about 400 different breeds in the world. On the next few pages you'll meet some of the most popular. But first, some pointers to help you pick the dog that's right for you.

Large?

Large dogs need lots of room, both indoors and out. Very large dogs, like the Saint Bernard, may even need an outdoor kennel. Big dogs have appetites to match their size. A St. Bernard for instance can easily gobble around 1 kg (2-3 lbs) of dry food, or 2.2 kg (5 lbs) of canned or meat rations a day.

Or Small?

Small dogs are suited to small houses and yards, but some, like terriers, are very energetic and will take great delight in digging up your garden. Small dogs may not eat much but they can be fussy about what they do eat. And some, like the Chihuahua, are just too fragile for playful rough-housing.

Who's Got the Time?

All dogs need exercise, training and grooming. But some, like the Labrador Retriever, bred for hunting, need more exercise than a quiet lapdog like the Pekingese. Long-haired breeds like the Afghan Hound need more brushing than short-haired varieties like the Dachshund.

And when it comes to training, some dogs, like the Golden Retriever, love to learn, while others, like the Pomeranian, seem to have a mind of their own.

Male or Female?

Some people think that female dogs are more affectionate and less aggressive than male dogs. And, usually, female dogs are smaller than male dogs and less likely to wander.

TOP DOGS

Find out who's for you in this who's who guide to the most popular dogs around today.

West Highland White Terrier
6.3-8.1 kg (14-18 lbs)
The "Westie" was bred in the western highlands of Scotland to hunt vermin.

Alaskan Malamute
34-39 kg (75-85 lbs)
Named for the Malamute tribe of Alaska, this sled dog has a thick, warm coat that suits it to life outdoors.

Boston Terrier
5.4-11.3 kg (12-25 lbs)
This polite, handsome dog with the smooth, easy-care coat has earned the nickname of "American gentleman."

Great Pyrenees
41-57 kg (90-125 lbs)
This huge and powerful dog was bred as an all-round worker—expert at everything from pulling carts to guarding sheep.

Doberman Pinscher
23-34 kg (50-75 lbs)
Originally bred as a fearless guard dog, the Doberman was the official war dog of the U.S. Marines during World War II. It makes an intelligent watchdog and a loyal pet.

Weimaraner
25-34 kg (55-75 lbs)
Nicknamed "Gray Ghost," this dog was bred in the early 1800s by Grand Duke Karl August of Weimar. Though it gained its reputation as a hunting dog, it also makes a friendly family pet.

Afghan Hound
23-27 kg (50-60 lbs)
This sleek, graceful hound not only needs daily grooming, but lots of exercise, as it was originally bred for speed as a desert hunter.

St. Bernard
57-80 kg (125-175 lbs)
This huge dog of avalanche rescue fame has an appetite to match its size. However, this giant makes a gentle pet.

Cairn Terrier
35.8-6.3 kg (13-14 lbs)
This shaggy little pet gets its name from being able to squeeze through the piles of stones, or "cairns" of Scotland

Basset Hound
13.6-25 kg (30-55 lbs)
This sad-looking dog made famous by Hush Puppy shoes has a super nose. As it was bred to trail and flush game, it needs a good daily walk.

Pekingese
3.1-6.3 kg (7-14 lbs)
Once the sacred dog of China, this tiny pet with the feathered tail and luxuriant coat is a favorite at dog shows.

Maltese
1.8-3.1 kg (4-7 lbs)
This dainty lapful was bred on the Mediterranean island of Malta centuries ago. It makes a lovable pet, but its silky coat needs careful attention.

Samoyed
16.3-30.3 kg (36-67 lbs)
Named for the Siberian tribe called the Samoyedes, this dog is a powerful sled dog. Its soft, white undercoat can be spun into yarn to make a fine-quality wool.

Fox Terrier
6.3-8.1 kg (14-18 lbs)
This cheerful pet was bred to hunt and drag foxes out of their dens. It comes in two varieties: wirehaired and smooth.

Keeshond
16-20 kg (35-45 lbs)
Originally from Holland, the Keeshond was known as the Dutch barge dog. Riverboat captains used them to guard barges and catch rats.

Airedale Terrier
18.1-27.2 kg (40-60 lbs)
This handsome dog is easy to train and makes a good pet. It was used as a battlefield messenger in World War I.

Schipperke
5.4-8.1 kg (12-18 lbs)
This Schipperke is small but strong. Its name means "Little Captain" in Flemish. It once guarded barges in its native Belgium.

Miniature Schnauzer
5.4-8.1 kg (12-18 lbs)
This gutsy little dog has a non-shedding coat and loves people. It's probably a cross between the standard Schnauzer and the Affenpinscher.

Vizsla
16-25 kg (35-55 lbs)
This powerful Vizsla is Hungary's most famous hunting dog. This expert pointer and retriever is also an affectionate friend.

English Springer Spaniel
18-25 kg (40-55 lbs)
This fine, all-round hunter is not only a highly successful show dog but a friendly pet.

Brittany Spaniel
13.6-18.4 kg (30-40 lbs)
This spaniel is unique for two reasons: unlike other spaniels it points to its game, and some are born with just a stub of a tail, if any at all!

Rottweiler
36.3-50 kg (80-110 lbs)
These dogs are descended from Roman cattle dogs. Because of their nature, they need a firm strong owner to keep them in order.

Lhasa Apso
6.8-9 kg (15-20 lbs)
Underneath that cascade of dense, straight hair is a loyal companion. It was originally bred in Tibet as a valuable guard dog.

Chesapeake Bay Retriever
25-34 kg (55-75 lbs)
A waterproof coat, webbed feet and a sturdy build make this dog a popular retriever among hunters.

Pomeranian
1.3-3.4 kg (3-7 lbs)
This frisky ball of fluff needs lots of grooming to keep it looking neat. It's a friendly little pet.

Silky Terrier
3.6-4.5 kg (8-10 lbs)
Underneath all that hair is a tiny, but excellent watchdog. Originally from Australia and hence nick-named "Sydney Silky" this dog makes a playful pet.

Bouvier Des Flandres
36.2-47.6 kg (80-105 lbs)
This sturdy dog loves to be active outdoors as it was once a farm dog in Northern France. Today it's used in police and guard work.

Shetland Sheepdog
6.8-9 kg (15-20 lbs)
This affectionate, obedient "Sheltie" has a thick coat bred for warmth in the days when it guarded sheep on the Shetland Islands.

Siberian Husky
15.9-27.2 kg (35-60 lbs)
This muscular husky is a hard-working dog of the north, but it makes a happy, affectionate pet almost anywhere.

Norwegian Elkhound
20.4-27.2 kg (45-60 lbs)
Bred to hunt elk in Scandinavia, this sturdy dog makes a loyal family pet, but it needs lots of freedom to run and exercise.

Miniature Pinscher
3-5 kg (7-11 lbs)
The "Min Pin" originated in Germany 300 years ago. This muscular little pet is an alert watchdog. Its smooth coat needs little attention.

German Shorthaired Pointer
20.4-31.8 kg (45-70 lbs)
This dog is a devoted and enthusiastic hunter that not only points and tracks but retrieves from land or water. Its webbed feet and water-repellent coat are an added bonus.

Pug
6-8 kg (14-18 lbs)
This dog from the Orient, was popular with 18th-century European ladies.

Bloodhound
36-50 kg (79-110 lbs)
The Bloodhound's nose is so sensitive that it can follow a scent from a single drop of blood.

All puppies begin life small—but they don't all stay small. If you are thinking about buying a dog find out how big it will grow. Here are some more dogs for you to look at.

Cardigan Welsh Corgi
7-12 kg (15-26 lbs)
A type of Corgi was used as a cattle dog by the ancient Celts who lived in Wales more than 3,000 years ago. The Corgi was so friendly that it often guarded children too.

Rhodesian Ridgeback
30-33.6 kg (66-74 lbs)
Bred 150 years ago for life in Africa, it can stand hot days and cold nights and lasts longer than most dogs without water.

English Cocker Spaniel (top)
Shorter American
10-15 kg (22-34 lbs)
The English Cocker probably came from Spain, hence its name. The American's ancestors were brought to North America in 1880.

Golden Retriever
27-34 kg (59-74 lbs)
This intelligent dog makes a fine, gentle pet. With its thick undercoat, this tough hunting dog can easily withstand the cold.

Bulldog
18-23 kg (40-50 lbs)
This former fighting dog was bred to attack bulls, bears, even lions. But that doesn't stop it from being a devoted pet.

Rough Collie
23-34 kg (50-74 lbs)
There are several types of Collies, but the most famous is the rough, or "Lassie" collie.

Poodle
3-25 kg (6-55 lbs)
The hunting Poodle was originally clipped so that its pompoms would keep it warm when it plunged into icy water after prey.

Irish Setter
27-32 kg (59-70 lbs)
A hunting dog must be agile, have a keen sense of smell and the ability to "point."

Bull Terrier
13.6-26.8 kg (30-59 lbs)
This dog is particularly friendly to familiar people. It needs a firm control, especially around other dogs.

Great Dane
55-68 kg (121-149 lbs)
Oddly enough, this beautiful gentle dog was bred not in Denmark but in Germany more than 400 years ago. It was first used for boar hunting, but now makes a fine companion.

Dalmatian
20-29 kg (45-65 lbs)
This dog rose to fame in England, first as a coach dog, then as a very popular firehouse dog. It makes a fine pet and watchdog.

Chihuahua
0.5-3 kg (1-6 lbs)
This tiny Mexican dog is a great watchdog. Its high-pitched bark warns of intruders approaching.

Scottish Terrier
8-10 kg (17-22 lbs)
Inside this high-spirited little dog is a big dog's bark. Along with its fearsome voice it has strong nails and a powerful jaw.

Irish Wolfhound
48-63 kg (105-138 lbs)
The tallest dog of all was the favorite of Irish Kings over 1,500 years ago.

Dachshund
2-9 kg (4-20 lbs)
This friendly, clean dog has powerful jaws, a keen sense of smell and loves to dig.

German Shepherd
27-39 kg (59-85 lbs)
Bred from several types of German sheep herding dogs, this intelligent, brave dog has proven itself a hero many times in police and rescue work.

Labrador Retriever
25-34 kg (55-75 lbs)
Because of this dog's strength and steady temperament, it's not only a good pet but an excellent guide and police dog. It has even learned to parachute from planes.

Old English Sheepdog
23-45 kg (50-100 lbs)
This good-natured, reliable "mop" is easy to train but needs lots of grooming to keep it looking its best.

Chow Chow
23-27 kg (50-59 lbs)
If you ever have trouble identifying this ancient Chinese hunting dog, look at its tongue. It's purple-black. This very independent dog is wary of strangers but is playful with its master.

Beagle
8-14 kg (17-30 lbs)
A merry pet and a very good hunter, this little dog used to be carried to the hunt in 16th-century England in saddle baskets.

Boxer
27-35 kg (59-77 lbs)
This sturdy Boxer is popular as a family pet, companion and watchdog. Its ears are naturally floppy unless they are cropped and trained to grow upright.

Basenji
10-11 kg (22-24 lbs)
Bred nearly 5,000 years ago by African bushmen for hunting and companionship the Basenji doesn't bark, and cleans itself like a cat.

Greyhound
27-32 kg (59-70 lbs)
Over 4,000 years ago this breed was trained by desert hunters to chase down small game. It can run at speeds up to 66 km/h (41 mph).

Yorkshire Terrier
2-4 kg (1-8 lbs)
It's hard to believe that this toylike dog with its silky hair tied back from its eyes was originally bred to kill rats in English factories 100 years ago. But it's true!

Newfoundland
50-69 kg (110-149 lbs)
This dog is so much at home in the water that it can both dive and swim under the surface. It has a water-shedding, oily coat and webbing between its toes.

PICKING A PUPPY

Who can resist the sweet little face and big, bright eyes of a puppy? Hardly anyone. But before you pick a puppy (or even a full-grown dog), consider these dos and don'ts...

DO

Find out all you can about the kind of dog you want. Read books, talk to other owners, visit breeders.

Buy from a breeder if you decide on a purebred dog. This way you have a chance to see the pup's mother and ask the breeder questions.

Pick a healthy dog, with bright, clear eyes; shiny coat; pink, firm gums.

Find out what shots, veterinary treatments, or dewormings the pup has had.

Watch the litter to see how all the puppies act when they're together. Clap your hands or make another loud noise and watch how the puppies react.

Pick the pup that's calm and interested in you.

DON'T
Choose a pup that isn't weaned from its mother. The best age to get a puppy is around seven weeks (49 days) old.

Choose the dog that cringes or acts nervous. It may make a very timid pet.

Choose the noisy one that barks or growls. It may be too difficult to train.

Bring a new pet home at Christmas or at any other festive occasion. The noise and excitement might make it hard for the dog to settle into its new home.

Choose a pup unless looks bright, alert and healthy.

BONING UP ON DOGS

How did our friendship with dogs begin? It happened in the days of the cave dwellers, probably something like this:

For many nights wolflike creatures crept closer and closer to the cave in hopes of snatching up any bones that were thrown outside. At first the cave dwellers were frightened of these shaggy creatures, but slowly the cavemen realized how useful these creatures were to them. Whenever other, more dangerous animals approached, the bone stealers growled or barked, both warning the people inside the cave and scaring away the intruders. Before long, the cave dwellers were capturing the pups of these helpful animals to raise and tame them. The partnership between people and dogs had begun.

24

Over the years, as dogs and early people came to know one another better, they began to work and hunt together. As time passed, people realized that certain dogs ran faster, caught prey better or were more diligent trackers. Slowly, by breeding dogs with desirable characteristics, people began creating dogs that had different sizes, shapes and abilities. Later, as people learned more about breeding, they began to develop special-purpose dogs: hunters, trackers, watchdogs, herd dogs, racing dogs, sled-pulling dogs and even cuddly pets. New types are still being developed every year.

THE DOG UP CLOSE

**To understand all dogs better
take a close-up look at this Husky...**

Dog Years
Nowadays, a well-cared for housepet that is not allowed to roam free will often live 15 years or longer. Unfortunately some breeds such as Giant Breeds have only a 10-12 year lifespan.

Most of a dog's growing up is done in the first two years of its life. So a two-year old dog, if it were a human, would be 24. From then on, one dog year equals four human years. So a three year-old dog would be 28, etc.

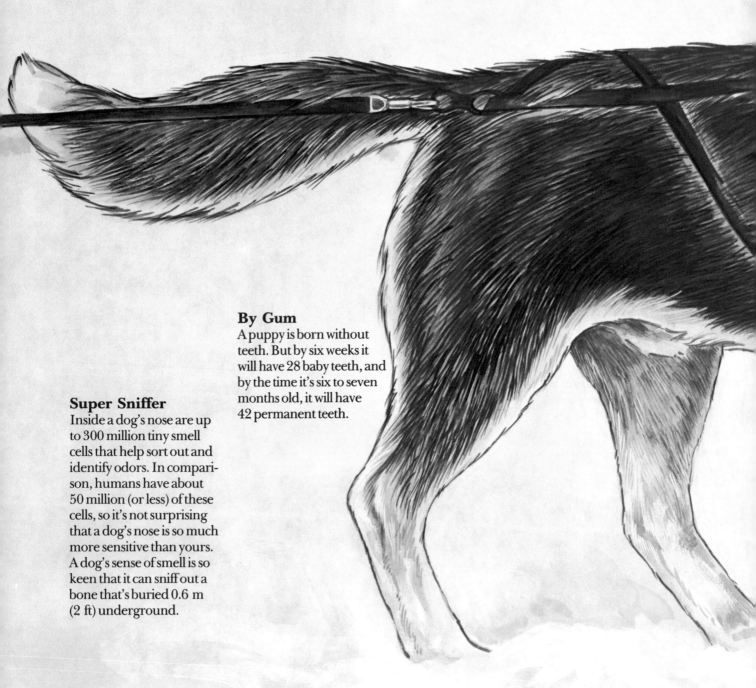

By Gum
A puppy is born without teeth. But by six weeks it will have 28 baby teeth, and by the time it's six to seven months old, it will have 42 permanent teeth.

Super Sniffer
Inside a dog's nose are up to 300 million tiny smell cells that help sort out and identify odors. In comparison, humans have about 50 million (or less) of these cells, so it's not surprising that a dog's nose is so much more sensitive than yours. A dog's sense of smell is so keen that it can sniff out a bone that's buried 0.6 m (2 ft) underground.

No Shouting, Please

Dogs can hear a noise a block away that a person wouldn't hear right next door. A dog can hear four times as well as you, but it's not quite as sensitive as a cat.

Shades of Gray

A dog has very limited color vision—if any at all. In fact, most scientists think that dogs see in various shades of gray—a bit like seeing the world on a black-and-white television set.

Useful Chompers

A dog's teeth are designed for grasping, tearing, shredding and shearing. But because a dog can't move its jaws sideways to grind food, it swallows its food in small chunks.

Nose Patch

The leatherlike nose pad you see on a dog is a protective covering for its sensitive smelling apparatus. Most often a dog's nose is cool and moist. A dog's nose can be warm and moist however, when it's over heated. In some circumstances, such as when a dog is not overheated and conserving water, it may be dry—and this is also normal.

Glow-in-the-Dark Eyes

Shine a light in your dog's eyes and you'd think there were mirrors inside. In a way that's right, because at the back of each eye is a layer of shiny cells that catches and magnifies any light coming in. These cells help your dog see better at night than you do.

SPECIAL DOGS

On these pages you'll meet some of the most interesting dogs bred over the years for special purposes.

The K-9 Corps

Dogs have been used in war since early Roman times. Then they were sent to battle wearing tiny suits of armor and huge spiked collars. Even in modern times, dogs have performed many important military tasks. During World War II, German Shepherds (nicknamed the K-9 Corps) carried coded messages in their collars and medical supplies and sniffed out poisonous gases. Doberman Pinschers became the official United States Marines dog and Labrador Retrievers were regularly parachuted behind enemy lines.

Super Herder

From the time man started to herd animals, dogs were used to ward off predators. One of the popular herding dogs is the Border Collie, bred hundreds of years ago near the border between Scotland and England. One of these hard-working dogs can herd as many as 1,000 sheep, and the herding instinct is so strong that collie pups will even try to herd children.

Sled Dogs

Even in prehistoric times dogs were used as partners in pulling heavy loads. And interestingly enough, the Siberian Huskies of Arctic sled-dog fame are direct descendants of that type of dog befriended by early cave dwellers (see page 24). Even today Huskies are very much like wolves in their behavior toward the dog that leads their team. They obey their "boss" unquestioningly.

Super Sniffer

Bloodhounds were bred by French bishops in the Middle Ages. Today, this gentle dog is renowned for a sense of smell so keen that it can pick up and follow a scent more than five days old.

Super Swimmer

The huge but gentle Newfoundland was bred more than 250 years ago on the Canadian island for which it is named. Webbed feet make the Newfoundland a powerful swimmer, and a thick coat keeps it cozy even in icy water. Newfoundlands once traveled on sailing ships and fishing boats to rescue any people who fell overboard and to haul big fishing nets from the water onto land.

Super Saluki

"My Saluki will catch gazelle even if they gallop over the stars," is an Arab boast almost as old as the Saluki dog itself. For countless centuries, desert sheiks hunted gazelle on horseback. On their wrists sat the falcons that would help make the catch, and on their saddles sat their Salukis, ready at the first glimpse of gazelle to streak through the air and give chase at speeds up to 64 km/h (40 mph). Even today, Arab Salukis are considered such special dogs that they are not for sale. When a Saluki dies, it is mourned as one of the family.

Rescue Dog

In the 1750s the monks of the Saint Bernard Hospice used a large dog (which was related to Mastiffs and Bloodhounds) to guide people and carry supplies through the Swiss Alps. When they discovered what a wonderful sense of smell these dogs had, they trained them to rescue travelers as well.

Sleeve Dogs

The Pekingese was unknown in Europe until after the first China War of 1860. When Franco-British forces invaded the Summer Palace in Peking, they discovered five of these snub-nosed dogs guarding the body of the emperor's aunt. She kept them as "sleeve dogs," as did most Chinese aristocrats, tucked up inside her loose sleeve to keep her warm. Now, that's a special-purpose dog.

Super Worker

Centuries ago, the monks of Tibet began writing prayers on pieces of parchment to put them into circular revolving boxes, or prayer wheels. The monks believed that all the while their prayer wheels turned, their prayers were being said. So they bred tiny Tibetan Spaniels to walk their treadmills. This, of course, took up a lot of a dog's day—but the monks' dogs still found time to serve as gutsy watchdogs as well as cozy lap warmers.

31

AMAZING BUT TRUE

YODEL-AH-EE-DEE

Does your dog cringe and try to hide under the bed during a thunderstorm? Some dogs do have noise phobias and are legitimately frightened of thunderstorms. A dog's hearing is so keen that it can hear thunder long before a person can. All that noise is very hard on sensitive ears.

Dalmatian puppies are born white. They start to get their spots when they are about five weeks old.

Can't make up your mind whether to get a dog or a cat as a pet? Then you might want to consider a Basenji. An ancient breed of dog that was pictured on Egyptian carvings 5,000 years ago, the Basenji cleans itself like a cat and doesn't bark. What noise does it make, you ask? It murmurs, chortles, snarls and even yodels.

When you pat, talk to, or are even near a dog (or a cat), you feel better, scientists say. Your blood pressure drops, and that's good for you.

The Xoloitzcuintli from Mexico is a completely hairless dog except for a bristly tuft on the top of its head. When you cuddle it it feels like a suede hot-water bottle!

According to the *Guinness Book of World Records*, the world's strongest dog is a Newfoundland named "Barbara-Allen's Dark Hans." At the 1979 Annual Bothell, Washington, Weight Pull, Hans pulled a weight of 2288.6 kg (5,045½ lbs). That's the same as you pulling a subcompact car.

Be careful where you step when a Chihuahua is around. That's because some are no bigger than a grapefruit.

If all dogs held a race, the winner would be the Greyhound. With its long legs and sleek body, it can reach a speed of 66 km/h (41 mph).

Who's the tallest dog of all? It's a toss-up. The Irish Wolfhound and the Great Dane both measure 99 cm (39 in) at the shoulder.

The next time you have a stomach ache, try putting a small dog on your lap to relieve the pain. That's what the women of ancient Rome did.

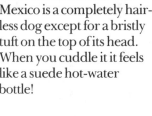

Most female dogs have between two and six puppies in a litter. But in June, 1944, a Foxhound named Lena surprised everyone with a litter of 23 puppies.

EYE SPY

Here are six pairs of eyes, each belonging to a different purebred dog. Can you identify each one by looking into its eyes? Turn the page and rate yourself as an eye-spy detective.

Here's looking at you...

Black Chow

Cairn

Old English Sheepdog

Australian Shepherd

Afghan

Shih Tzu

TATTLE TAILS

Attached to these tails are six purebred dogs. How many can you identify? Turn the page to see the completed pictures.

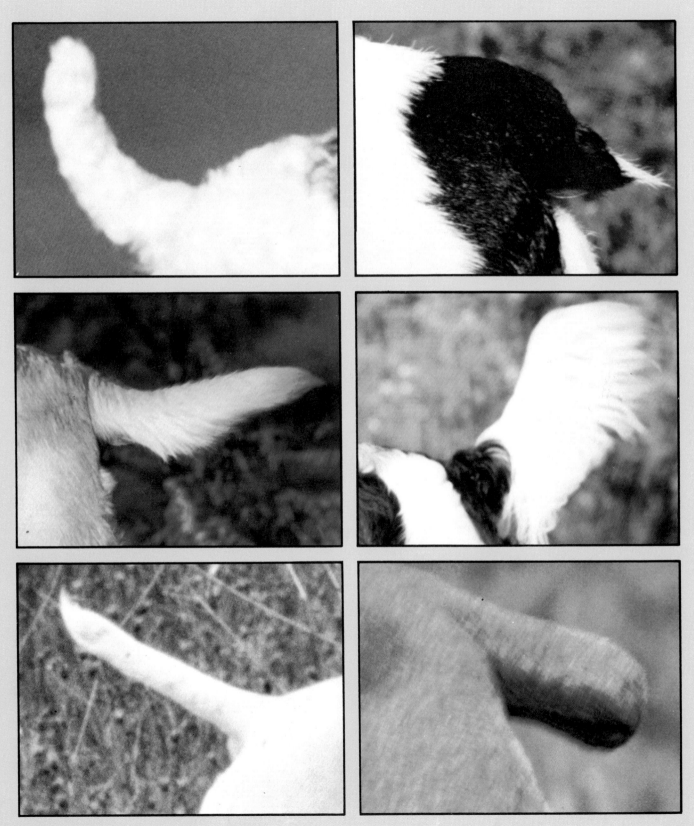

The tail end...

Boxer

Pointer

Wire Fox Terrier

French Bulldog image

French Bulldog

Springer Spaniel

Yellow Labrador

AMAZING BUT TRUE

The coyote is probably the fastest wild canid of all. It can reach speeds of up to 65 km/h (40 mph).

Coyotes usually hunt alone, but sometimes two will team up together to grab a meal. One coyote will try to distract a rabbit or other prey by running around in circles or jumping up and down. This gives the second coyote the perfect chance to sneak up and pounce on the unsuspecting prey.

One of the world's oddest dogs is the Raccoon Dog of Northern Europe. It's the only member of the Canid family that hibernates. It doesn't bark or even howl. But it does growl, whimper and even meows. Meows! Yes, and it can swallow eight to 10 trout-sized fish in rapid succession.

Why does the red fox have a white tip on the end of its tail? The better to talk with, of course. Like all members of the dog family, the fox uses its tail to communicate. And the white tip makes sure that the tail is "heard."

Hawks foolhardy enough to swoop down after new born jackals are in for a nasty surprise. Adult jackals will jump up into the air and bite them.

You can't get much bigger than a wolf, in wild Canid circles, that is. A male wolf can weigh up to 77 kg (170 lbs), with paws measuring 15 cm (6 in) across!

The only time a wolf has a safe home that it can crawl into is during the first few months of its life. After that, it lives and sleeps outside with the rest of the pack.

A gray fox, unlike other dogs, has no trouble scurrying up trees. Why? It has sharp, curved claws, much like a cat's.

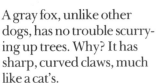

The fennec, a fox that lives in the Sahara desert, has huge ears. Not only are they built-in air conditioners that help the fox lose some of its body heat, but they also help the fox hear the tiny insects it hunts and eats.

In spite of their name and even though they can bark, prairie dogs are not dogs at all. They're ground squirrels.

A wolf's howl is one of the most beautiful and exciting sounds of nature. Howling is a wolf's way of talking to other pack members while hunting or warning other wolves to stay away, or keeping in touch when separated from the pack. And sometimes a wolf will throw back its head and howl just for the joy of it. Its voice will carry 5 km (3 miles). What a song!

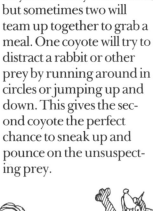

37

Nick, Sophia and Mark Mite are three special kids with a big secret: they have discovered a way to shrink to any size they want, and grow big again. If they shrink small enough they can float on air, even stay underwater for as long as they wish. The Mites are at home one day when they notice that their dog, Bricks, is scratching more than usual. They decide to investigate the cause...

by Emily Hearn and Mark Thurman

MIGHTY MITES
ON A SHAGGY DOG

LISTEN TO BRICKSIE HE SURE DOES HAVE LOUD DREAMS!

IS THAT WHY HE'S TWITCHING SO MUCH?

GGRRR GRRR

MAYBE SOMETHING'S BITING HIM.

WE COULD SHRINK AND FIND OUT.

THE MITES SHRINK

IF BRICKSIE COULD SEE US NOW...

HE'D HAVE A NIGHTMARE.

HEE-HEE!

ZZZZZZZ

FAMILY TREE

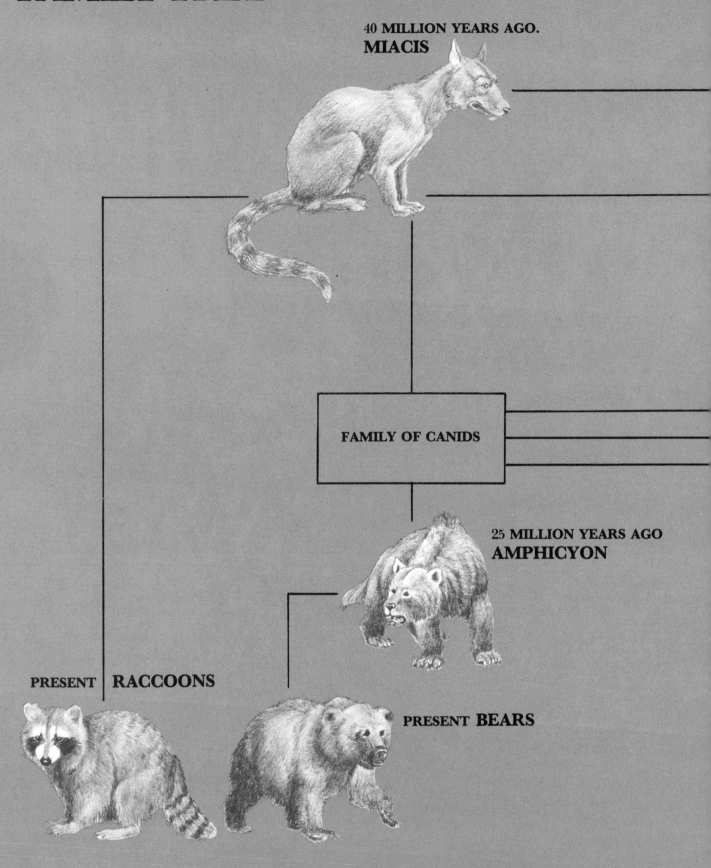

40 MILLION YEARS AGO.
MIACIS

FAMILY OF CANIDS

25 MILLION YEARS AGO
AMPHICYON

PRESENT **RACCOONS**

PRESENT **BEARS**

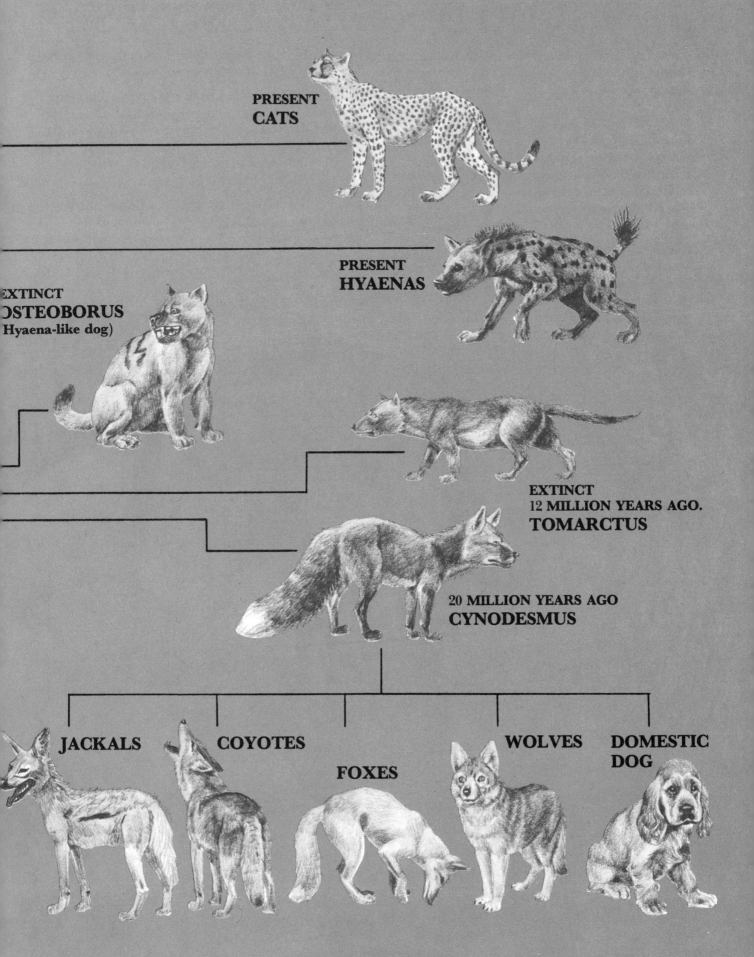

PRESENT
CATS

PRESENT
HYAENAS

EXTINCT
OSTEOBORUS
(Hyaena-like dog)

EXTINCT
12 MILLION YEARS AGO.
TOMARCTUS

20 MILLION YEARS AGO
CYNODESMUS

JACKALS   COYOTES   WOLVES   DOMESTIC
                                                      DOG
                    FOXES

WHY DO DOGS BURY BONES?

This very minute, somewhere in the world, wild cousins of the friendly "family" dog are probably hunting a deer to eat. They work as a team as they chase the animal, bring it to the ground and kill it. Then they tear into its flesh, gulping down huge hunks as fast as they can while keeping an eye out for approaching danger. When all the meat is gone, they begin to gnaw on some bones and bury others. The leader will start to walk away when he feels it's time to leave, and the others will follow.

Members of the *Canid* family have behaved like this for millions of years. They obey their pack leader, which makes their hunt organized; they are watchful for intruders who might steal their precious meal; they eat in a hurry because there is not always enough food to go around; and they bury their bones so they can return to chew on them when hunting is bad.

Once you know about dogs' strong and ancient instincts, pet dogs become even more fascinating. When they turn circles before lying down on the smooth kitchen floor, they are going through the same motions as their wild relatives, who do this to make a soft place in long grass.

When dogs urinate on trees and bushes, they are marking off the boundaries of their territory, leaving a "keep out" sign for other Canid packs, even though domestic dogs don't need hunting territories.

One of the dog's strongest instincts — loyalty to the pack leader and willingness to follow and obey — is responsible for its unique relationship with people. A dog thinks of its owner as the pack leader and this is why it tries so hard to please. When your dog rolls over, belly up, in front of you, it is telling you that it knows you're its master. Being a dog's best friend is quite a responsibility.

One of the dog's earliest instincts is to root. A puppy — wild or domestic — will nudge its nose closer and closer to its mother looking for milk. When your dog nudges you with its nose, it's following the same instinct. But instead of milk, your dog is looking for attention and affection.

A puppy will also press its front paws against its mother's teat to make the milk flow. When your dog lifts its paw up to you, it's saying it wants to be friends.

Dog owners are very happy about one instinct that all dogs share: a desire to keep their dens clean. All dogs — from the wolf to your pet dog — hate to soil their living area. Even puppies, once they are old enough, will stagger out of their box to relieve themselves. It's because of this ancient instinct that dogs can be easily housebroken.

DOG LANGUAGE

Dogs communicate by sound and action. And dog "street talk" isn't much different from wolf "wild talk" (when you know the language.)

When two strange dogs meet for the first time they usually circle one another very slowly. Each one tries to make itself look bigger by holding its tail high and arching its neck. The fur along the neck and backbone might even stand on end.

If one dog lets the other sniff its tail or rolls over on its back, it is saying "I give in." If neither dog gives in, they may start to fight. They will push at each other's shoulders, growl and try to get the other to the ground. They may even attack each other's throats and muzzles.

When two dogs that are friends meet, they will stand head to tail sniffing each other's bodies.

When a dog feels playful, it will lift its paw or may even "bow" down, holding its rump in the air and wagging its tail wildly.

When a dog wants to say "I'm sorry," it will turn its head sideways and bare its neck. It may even crouch down, wag its tail slowly and lift its front paw a little.

Dogs do smile and it's usually with their mouths open and their tongues out. A dog's smile is a submissive sign of greeting and it means, "I want to play."

Watch out for a dog that draws back its lips and growls. It's angry. Usually a dog will stop growling just before it attacks.

Ear positions can mean many things depending on the other facial expressions and body postures. Ears back can mean angry, frightened, defensive or nervous. Ears up—concentrating dog! Ears forward, it's on the alert.

49

TELL TAILS

**All these dogs are
talking with their tails.
Here's what they're saying.**

**1. Tail held high
and wagging**
I'm happy.

**3. Tail held low
without moving.**
I'm insecure.

2. Tail held still
I'm unsure.

**4. Tail held down
between legs**
I give in.

PET PEEVES

These dogs are speaking up for millions of others about things people do that bug dogs most.

A DOG WHATSIT

Hopping Huskies and leaping Lhasas! Here's a dog we hope that you never see. That's because it's made up of six different breeds. A Bouvier des Flandres, a Chow Chow, an Irish Setter, a Poodle, a Standard Schnauzer and a Welsh Corgi are all involved — but how?

Answer on page 96

SUPER DOGS

Meet some dog heroes that have shown their friendship to humans in very special ways.

CANDY IS DANDY

Candy, a bloodhound from Saranac, N.Y., did something that close to 200 people before her had tried to do but failed: she found an eight-year-old autistic boy who was lost in dense woods. What made the job so difficult was that almost four days had passed since the boy was first missing and in the meantime there had been heavy rains and cold temperatures. The ground had also been trampled by hundreds of searchers. But Candy took one good whiff of the air and was hot on the trail. She soon found the boy, asleep but safe, in the thick underbrush.

FIRE RESCUE

Sheba, the eight-year-old German Shepherd, lost her sight in February, 1979, while rescuing a Miniature Poodle and trying to save four parakeets from her owner's Toronto, Canada home — an act that earned her the title of the Ontario Humane Society's "Hero of the Year."

When fire broke out, Sheba grabbed Brandy, a Poodle, by the neck and carried it outdoors. Despite the smoke and flames, Sheba went back into the burning building to save the parakeets and was almost to the door when the floor gave way. Alas, the birds disappeared into the fire but Sheba was dragged to safety by her owner. Sheba's story has a happy ending. This brave dog regained her sight a few months later.

HELPFUL EARS

This dog isn't leaping onto his owner's bed for a playful romp. He's a special dog with a special owner. This dog is a Hearing Dog that was trained to be his deaf master's ears. So he will jump onto the bed to tell his master that the alarm clock is ringing and that it's time to get up. He will also alert him when a visitor comes to the door, the telephone rings, the smoke detector sounds and even when the baby cries. The American Humane Society started the Hearing Dog Project in 1976. Its dogs come in all sorts of different shapes, sizes and breeds — but their orange collars and leashes tell you that they are working dogs with a job to be done.

TV SHOW DOG

What's it like for a dog to be a TV star? A number of years ago when a show called *The Littlest Hobo* was regularly being filmed, our reporter went out to watch some scenes. Here's what she saw on the farm where the film crew was getting ready to shoot.

What a mess! The field was a tangle of cables and wires running from two large vans full of TV equipment. There were about 20 people at work wheeling around large lights on tall stands, testing sound equipment or fiddling with huge cameras.

Suddenly someone shouted, "Quiet on the set." Two actors took their places near a tent. One of them was holding a gun. As Hobo and his owner, Charles Eisenmann, walked onto the set, I crept closer to see what was happening.

"Bo," the dog's owner said, "I want you to circle around behind the man with the gun, sneak slowly up and pause. Then I want you to jump up and hit him on his back without hurting him so he'll fall forward."

I was amazed. How could a dog possibly understand such difficult instructions? As soon as the director yelled, "Action," we found out. Mr. Eisenmann stood behind the camera, quietly talking to Hobo. "Okay, Bo, come forward...slow... slow...hold it! Now jump." Just as he said that, Hobo leapt at the gunman, striking him with his front paws. The gunman fell on the ground and the other actor ran away.

"Cut. Perfect!" yelled the director, and the scene was over. The gunman and Hobo tussled playfully for a minute, then sat up to see what the director wanted next.

While the crew was setting up for the next scene, I decided to visit Hobo in his motor home, which was parked nearby. Imagine a whole motor home for a dog! But the biggest surprise was yet to come. As Mr. Eisenmann opened the door, *five* Hobos jumped out! Mr. Einsenmann explained. Two are "stunt dogs" that stand in for Hobo when the script calls for a lot of running or jumping. One is a young dog training to be an actor, and another is too old to act any more but enjoys being part of the team.

I was still trying to tell the dogs apart when in came Megan Follows, the 14-year-old heroine of the show. "Oooh," she sighed, "air conditioning. You can sure tell who the star is around here." Then one of the Hobos behaved just like a movie star — he gave her a big, wet kiss.

Before we had much time to talk, someone yelled, "Makeup!" and we headed back to the set. In the next scene Hobo had to rescue Megan from a muddy cave-in. The technicians were going to set off three sticks of dynamite in a deep ditch to create the right effect. That meant there would be a lot of noise, smoke and flying dirt.

When Mr. Eisenmann had given Hobo careful instructions for the scene, the cameras were ready to roll. Boom! Up went the dynamite. Right on cue, without a moment's hesitation, Hobo hurled himself into the midst of a rising cloud of smoke.

Somehow he found the end of a rope in the ditch and leapt out, pulling it. Astounded by his speed and skill, the crew burst into applause.

I, too, was impressed by Hobo's performance. He seemed to be able to follow every instruction Charles Eisenmann gave him. "Can any dog learn to do this?" I later asked Mr. Eisenmann. "Yes," he replied, "but you have to be willing to work hard and learn to respect as well as love your dog." Then he told me his secret.

"To train your dog to follow your orders, you first have to teach him or her to understand what you're saying." Mr. Eisenmann taught Hobo words one by one by showing him that each word stands for something. Today Hobo understands so many words he can do almost anything he's asked to.

Can you learn to teach *your* dog to understand you? Turn to page 60 for some practical tips from Mr. Eisenmann.

WHO'S TRAINING WHO?

Most dogs are eager to learn if someone will spend the time to teach them. Here are a few teaching ideas from dog trainer Charles Eisenmann. First, two commands to get you and your dog started. When you've mastered them, turn the page for some more advanced commands.

"Come on, Rover, come to me!"

The idea here is first to catch your dog's interest and then match its actions with your command.

1. Begin teaching this command by taking your dog's favorite toy and walking three steps away.

2. Hold its toy out in front of you and *as your dog starts to move toward you* call, "Come on, Rover (or whatever your dog's name is), come to me."

3. When it comes, immediately praise it for doing well and give it a hug. *Don't give it the toy.*

4. Keep repeating all the steps until you don't need to use the toy any longer. Your dog will come when it's called because it understands that you want it to.

Before giving your dog a new command, pretend you are your pet. Would you have problems carrying out the command?

Try not to use food as a reward. You'll end up with a fat dog.

Never give your dog one- or two-word commands. Talk to it in sentences and eventually it will learn your language.

"Sit down, Rover. Please sit down!"
Like all attempts to teach your dog, this one requires patience. Your dog has to learn to hear and remember your command before it can do what you expect of it.

1. Start by standing close to your dog and holding its favorite toy just above its nose. The idea is to make this such an awkward position for it to stand in that it will automatically sit down.

2. *As it starts to sit*, say, "Sit down, Rover. Please sit down." Reward it the instant it sits with words of praise and a hug. *Don't give it the toy.*

3. If your dog backs up rather than sitting down, try again when it has a wall behind it so that it can't move backwards.

4. Repeat all the steps until your dog sits on command.

Getting to know each other better is half the fun of dog school. Your dog will learn faster if the same person teaches it all the time.

Be patient. Wait until your dog completely understands one command before going on to the next.

Keep classes short — no more than a minute long. After a 15-minute break, most dogs are ready to try again.

WHO'S TEACHING WHO?

Helping your dog learn some "showy" tricks is no more difficult than training it to obey basic commands. All you have to do is watch for it to do what you want, then teach it the words for what it's already doing.

"Bow down, Rover!"

1. Watch your dog when it wakes up from a nap.

2. When you see it begin to stretch, say, "Bow, down, Rover. That's a good boy." Repeat the word "bow" many times when it's stretching.

3. Praise it.

4. Every time you see your dog begin to stretch, repeat your command and reward it. Soon it will bow when you ask it to.

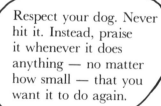

Learn to observe your dog carefully so that the moment you see it begin to do what you want, you can follow it up with the correct command.

You can start to train your puppy to obey basic commands (come-sit-stay, etc.) when it is six weeks old, but don't be disappointed if it's slow to learn. Wait until at least seven months old before you start to teach it to think for itself by increasing its vocabulary.

Respect your dog. Never hit it. Instead, praise it whenever it does anything — no matter how small — that you want it to do again.

"Pick it up, Rover!"

1. Throw your dog's ball or other favorite toy a very short distance — never more than four feet (1.3 m).

2. As it grabs for it, say, "Pick it up, Rover. Good boy." If it doesn't grab for it, throw it again. Watch your dog carefully. As soon as it moves toward the ball, give it the command, "Pick it up."

3. Praise it the moment it picks up the ball. Repeat all three steps many times until you're sure your dog understands what you mean by, "Pick it up."

4. Replace the ball with another object — for instance, an old hat — and ask your dog to pick it up. Then do it again with something else, perhaps an old shoe.

"Pick up the hat, Rover!"

Now that your dog understands the action command, "Pick it up," it's ready to learn what it is it's picking up.

1. Put its ball, the hat and the shoe on the ground in front of the dog.

2. On the command, "Pick it up," the dog will pick up its favorite — the ball. When it does, praise it.

3. Put the ball back on the ground and this time say, "Pick up the ball, Rover." Praise your dog when it does. Repeat this step several times. Put the ball away.

4. Give the dog the "Pick it up" command again and watch which of the two remaining objects it picks up. Let's say it's the hat. After praising the dog, put the hat back on the ground and say, "Pick up the hat, Rover." Reward your dog when it does, then repeat this step several times before putting the hat away.

5. Repeat what you did with the ball and the hat until your dog learns the word "shoe."

Dogs — like people — can't concentrate when there are too many distractions.

The most important ingredient in training sessions is love.

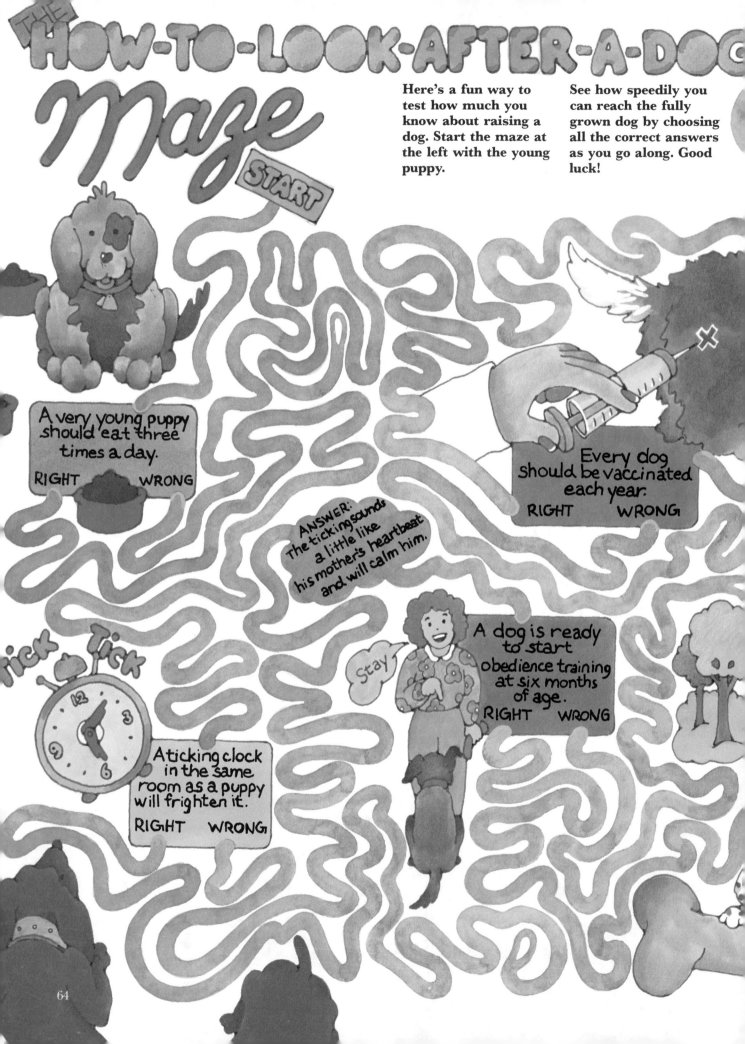

THE HOW-TO-LOOK-AFTER-A-DOG Maze

START

Here's a fun way to test how much you know about raising a dog. Start the maze at the left with the young puppy.

See how speedily you can reach the fully grown dog by choosing all the correct answers as you go along. Good luck!

A very young puppy should eat three times a day.
RIGHT   WRONG

Every dog should be vaccinated each year.
RIGHT   WRONG

ANSWER: the ticking sounds a little like his mother's heartbeat and will calm him.

Tick   Tick

A ticking clock in the same room as a puppy will frighten it.
RIGHT   WRONG

Stay

A dog is ready to start obedience training at six months of age.
RIGHT   WRONG

LOOKING AFTER YOUR DOG

A dog can be a wonderful family pet, providing its owner knows how to keep it healthy and happy. These are big responsibilities, but here are some tips to help.

Grooming Time

Too many baths can dry out a dog's skin and make it itchy. The best way to keep your dog clean is with regular grooming. Ask your vet which comb, brush and grooming glove is best for your dog.

First, comb your dog's coat to loosen tangles and dirt, then brush from head to tail to get rid of dead hair. Finally, shine the coat and massage the skin with a grooming glove.

Before brushing or combing any long-haired breed, lightly mist the coat with water. This will stop static electricity.

Get rid of pesky burrs without hurting your dog's coat by putting a bit of hair cream rinse or petroleum jelly on them before combing them out.

Check your dog's paw pads regularly for any stuck pebbles or stones. In winter, wipe any ice balls or salt from paws.

Even a puppy should be groomed—even if it means only a quick brush. This way it will get used to regular grooming and may even start to look forward to it.

Bath Time

If your dog gets so filthy that grooming alone can't get it clean, then it's time for a bath.

Always brush the dog vigorously before putting it into the water. This will help loosen the dirt and get rid of matted hair.

For a successful bath, you'll need: a nonskid mat to give your dog a firm footing in the basin or tub, a handheld shower attachment or small buckets to dip and pour water, dog shampoo, and towels. If your dog is frisky, secure it with a leash so it can't jump out of the tub.

Wet the dog well with warm water, and start soaping it up at the neck and work down to its tail.

Most dogs hate getting water on their faces, so wash the head last.

Rinse well so there's no soap left. Your dog could get sick from licking a soapy coat.

You can dry your dog quickly by using a blow hair dryer. But use the dryer only on the low setting and hold it away from its skin.

If your dog is skunked, a bath in tomato juice will help get rid of the stink. Let the juice dry on the dog and then brush it out. Never use a water bath. Your vet may also recommend a commercial product.

Dinner Time

No matter how often you groom your dog, its coat won't have that healthy shine if it isn't eating right. Talk to your vet about the best food for your dog.

Grown up dogs need only one meal a day. Puppies have tinier tummies, so they must eat at least two small meals a day.

Dogs enjoy routine, so feed your dog from the same dish and in the same place, around the same time each day.

Always leave out a dish of fresh drinking water for your dog.

Help keep your dog's teeth clean by giving it dry dog foods or biscuits, and chewy toys made of rawhide or nylon. Never give bones that can splinter easily.

Exercise Time

Daily workouts will keep your dog fit and trim. But it's best not to exercise right after meal time. Give your dog a chance to digest his food. Then it can run, swim, play catch and fetch or even a wild game of Frisbee. For more exercise ideas, see page 83.

WHAT IT'S LIKE
TO LIVE IN A DOGHOUSE

Dogs don't mind being put in the "doghouse," providing it is comfortable and cozy. Here are some tips from a dog's point of view on how to improve a dog's home (and furnishings).

This house is tops. It's off the ground, away from moisture and drafts. It's small enough that I can keep it warm with my body heat in cold weather, yet big enough that I can stretch out without stubbing my paws. The flap over the door and the sloping roof keep out rain and the straw makes a comfortable, warm bed.

FIDO

This choke chain makes a great training collar.

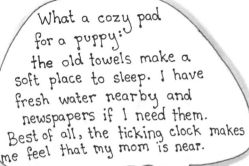

What a cozy pad for a puppy! the old towels make a soft place to sleep. I have fresh water nearby and newspapers if I need them. Best of all, the ticking clock makes me feel that my mom is near.

I can easily chew this sponge ball to bits, and what's worse is that I can swallow some of the pieces. I'd like a toy meant for dogs. How about a leather dog bone?

This leash is about 1.8m (6 ft.) long-- just long enough for me to walk comfortably ahead of my master. And unlike the chain leashes, this leather leash is not too heavy.

Uh, oh! This bed's too small. All I really need for a comfortable night's sleep is either a piece of carpet or a blanket on the floor.

Dogs with long noses need deep dishes. This dish is meant for a flat faced, short-nosed dog like my friend, the Pug.

You should be able to fit one or two fingers between my neck and collar. But this collar is so big that I can easily slip my head out. And by the way, where are my dog license and ID tags?

Want to trade?

ALBERT MY DOG

The swimmer at the right is Farley Mowat, author of Never Cry Wolf, A Whale for the Killing, The Dog Who Wouldn't Be and several other books you may have read. The creature swimming with him is Albert, Farley's Newfoundland Water Dog — a rare, smart and very unusual dog.

When Albert died, Farley wrote some memories of him. It was a good way, he said, to feel a little less sad.

I'll tell you what kind of a dog Albert was. Once, a few years ago, I left him with my father Angus in a cabin north of Kingston, Ontario, Canada. Albert was pretty happy there. But one night I happened to be giving a radio interview, and Albert heard me on the radio. And on this broadcast, I was talking about Albert. I said he was a great dog, and I said that I really missed not having him with me. Well, Angus let him out the door that night for his usual walk — but this time Albert disappeared. He was missing for eight days. He was finally discovered on the outskirts of Kingston. He'd run into some sort of trouble with a farm dog and he'd been chewed up a bit, and he was sort of healing his wounds. But there's no question about where he was heading; he was heading back to Newfoundland, hundreds of miles away. From the radio, Albert thought I'd gone back to our home in Newfoundland, you see, so he was on his way to join me.

Albert had a terrific imagination. He loved it when I told him stories. I have a sneaking suspicion that he could even read a bit — the large print, anyway. I found him occasionally staring at the headlines in newspapers. But he certainly loved to have stories told to him or read to him, and the more exciting they were, the better. The stories I used to tell him always ended up with a lion or a crocodile or a boa constrictor getting hold of Albert and eating him up. When I'd tell the story, Albert would start talking as soon as the story began — and as we came to the punch line, his growls would reach a crescendo.

I'm not kidding when I say that Albert was a great talker. He talked all the time. None of us realized until a short time ago that he really was talking. We'd say, "Listen to that crazy dog talk." He'd be growling and barking in the strangest way — but now it turns out that he really *was* talking, and we just weren't listening.

Albert never let a day go by without doing some hard work. He'd go down to the beach and collect firewood and then bring it back and stack it beside the house. He felt he had to contribute. He felt he was in partnership with us, not just a pet. But he never whined, never complained. He died of a heart attack, and the vet told us that the pain must have been colossal. But Albert never let on in any way. He was an incredibly brave dog, all his life, no matter what happened.

Albert entered my life when he was about four months old, when my wife Claire and I were living in Burgeo, Newfoundland. He was a Newfoundland Water Dog, which is a very special breed. *Very* special, because as far as I know, Albert was one of the last of his breed.

By the time Claire and I went to live there, there were hardly any Water Dogs left. We saw one or two dogs jumping into the water off the steamer dock. They were diving to the bottom to get bones and things that the cooks on the steamers threw overboard. They could stay under for minutes at a time!

Claire and I were fascinated, so we tried to find one of our own. But there weren't any pups. Finally, we found one dog who was about to have pups — and that's how we got Albert.

From what I can find out from my own research it seems that the breed originated among the Basque people in central Iberia, which is now Spain. In early times, when the Basques were driven to the seacoast by new people invading their homeland, they took their dogs with them — and the dogs adapted to the water.

Now the Basque people were great sailors, and they started coming from Europe to fish in Newfoundland as early as 1458. And they brought the dogs with them. It was a sort of fishing partnership. One dog went in every boat, and they did all kinds of useful work. For instance, they'd carry a line ashore, with the rope in their mouths, when the sea was so rough that people wouldn't.

These dogs — like many land mammals before them — headed back to the sea. They became fully aquatic, almost like a whale or a seal. And over the thousands of years that these dogs lived in the sea, their bodies developed special adaptations. They had webbed feet. They had long, heavy, muscular tails, which they used like a rudder on a boat. They developed very heavy forequarters and very light hindquarters, which allowed them to cut through the water like a boat. They developed thick hair on their backs that gave them buoyancy. And their necks were set at right angles to their bodies, and their heads at right angles to their necks, so that when they were swimming in heavy water, they could keep their heads above to breathe. They were the only dog that had any of these adaptations. The dogs that now have webbed feet all derived from the Water Dog.

I'll give you an example of how these dogs worked in the sea. Once a friend of mine was swimming, and pretended to be drowning. Albert turned and went for this young guy like a bullet. He raced out to him, then sort of put his brakes — and put his tail right in my friend's face! My friend realized what Albert was doing, so he simply grabbed his tail, and Albert towed him ashore.

71

TRAVELS WITH FIDO

**Dogs love to get out and about and see new
sights. Here are some tips to make
traveling with your dog more enjoyable....**

1. Plan several short drives before the long trip to
get your dog used to riding in a car. Even if your
dog never gets carsick, don't feed it for six to seven
hours before the trip.

3. Depending on the size of your pet and your
car, you may want your dog to ride in a special
pet traveling crate.

4. Make your dog feel more at home by packing
its favorite food and water bowls, a supply of its
usual food, a big Thermos jug of water, its
sleeping pad or blanket, its brush, and — of
course — its favorite toy.

2. Take your dog in and out of the car on a leash
and, if possible, train it to get in and out on
command. This way it won't jump out of the car
as soon as the door is open.

5. What should your dog never travel without?
Health and rabies certificates, ID tags, leash, the
name of a local vet if it plans to stay in one place
for a week or more, a color photograph of itself to
help you find it in case it is lost or stolen.

6. Don't let your dog hang its head out the window when it's in the car. Grits of sand or dirt can get in its eyes and nose. That can hurt!

7. Plan to stop the car every few hours for rest and exercise breaks.

8. Never leave your dog alone in the car, especially in very hot weather. But if you must, leave the car windows slightly open for ventilation.

9. Let the manager of any hotel or motel where you are staying know in advance that you will be bringing your dog along.

10. If you are planning to travel by train, boat or plane, check with the railways, shipping companies and airlines about the best arrangements to make for your dog.

WHEN THE WOLVES SANG

No one in the world knows wolves like Bill Mason. He has camped in the wilderness among wolves that have never seen a human being before and has raised wolf cubs at his family home. This story is based on one of his trips to the North to photograph wolves.

As the wolves moved along the wind-swept ridge, the crisp snow crunched beneath their feet. They were traveling at an easy lope, strung out single file behind their two leaders. Suddenly, on the brow of the hill, the male leader stopped, his breath hanging on the morning air and his steely coat glinting in the rising sun. His mate moved up beside him and also stopped. They both saw a herd of caribou resting in the middle of the lake ahead.

Sensing the excitement of the hunt, the followers in the pack clustered together. They were anxious to begin but dared not run ahead of the leaders. At last the wolves came down onto the ice and crossed the lake, angling away from the caribou. But the caribou were not fooled. They knew they were being hunted, but they waited and watched, saving their strength for the tremendous burst of speed they'd need to escape those powerful jaws.

The pack was about halfway from shore when suddenly the male leader stopped and looked toward the distant horizon. He could faintly hear a whining sound that did not belong to the forest. Now the rest of the pack heard it too, but because the leaders showed only mild interest, they were not afraid. They all stood gazing at the sky as a large bird flew into sight.

It was only when the bird came toward the pack that the wolves became nervous. Their tails dipped and their ears moved back against their heads. The leaders started to run for the trees at the edge of the lake and the pack followed. But then the noisy creature swung in a wide circle between the wolves and the safety of the shore. The wolves huddled uneasily around the leaders, wondering what to do next. Then the bird turned away, swooped down and landed on the lake among the caribou. As it came to rest, the noise stopped and silence returned to the land.

From the side of the great bird stepped another strange creature. The wolves had never seen anything like this before. It walked on only two legs and it stood there alone as the bird began to roar louder than ever. Again the pack broke into a run. As the bird lifted into the sky, the sound died away and the wolves turned to stare at the intruder.

It was *me* there on the ice, and as I blinked against the glare of the sun, as the plane that delivered me to this wild place flew away. I could hardly believe what I was seeing.

After weeks of searching, here I was alone among wild wolves. I quickly grabbed my camera with its long telephoto lens and focused on what looked like the leader, a huge gray wolf with a magnificent bushy tail. As I watched him, I shivered. But I knew I was safe because for some mysterious reason, wolves always avoid people.

After looking me over, the big wolf turned and climbed onto a small rocky island. Two others followed him and, after nuzzling each other, curled up and went to sleep. Then the rest of the pack lay down.

Now was the time to build an igloo. The packed snow was ideal, and the work went quickly. I had been working on my snow house for several hours when all of a sudden I looked up. The wolves on the rocky island were getting to their feet and, much to my surprise, instead of moving toward the rest of their pack, they started coming toward me. I quickly reminded myself that wolves aren't supposed to attack people. And I hoped these wolves knew that too!

At a distance that was just a little too close for comfort, the wolves stopped. Then, with one last glance at me, they turned toward the caribou. I realized that the wolves had only been working their way into position for the chase and I had been in the way. The caribou watched as the wolves approached. They stood motionless, but I knew they were ready to run.

Suddenly the big wolf charged! Immediately the lake was alive with hundreds of running caribou. They moved in a great wave, fanning out and away from the charging wolves. The wolves had almost caught up and were watching the herd for stragglers or a caribou that was limping. But there was none. The chase was over, and the caribou had escaped. I watched the wolves disappear among the trees on the far shore.

The lake seemed strangely still and suddenly I felt lonely. And then, in the distance, I heard a long, mournful howl. As more wolves joined in, the song grew and grew.

I thought about that song later as I lay in my igloo in the warm glow of candlelight. It was a song of terrible hunger and hardship, but it was also a song of hope and survival. And it was the most beautiful song I had ever heard. I would remember it forever.

CHIPEE PULLS THROUGH

Husky dogs have been pulling people all over the Arctic for the past 2,000 years. But today they are being replaced by faster snowmobiles. Today in the Canadian Arctic there are now fewer than 200 Husky dogs at work. Here is photographer-writer Fred Bruemmer's story of one dog.

Chipee was big and mischievous — you could even say troublesome — and he liked to fight. Usually, he didn't even get scratched, but finally a time came when he limped away from battle. One of Chipee's paws was badly hurt, but it couldn't have hurt him any more than what happened next.

That day we were leaving on a hunting trip, and all the dogs howled for joy when they saw the sleds being loaded. Chipee was howling too, but for a different reason. Because of his injured foot, he was chained up — and he knew very well that this meant he would not be going along. George Hakungak, Chipee's owner, told me that having to stay behind in camp is the worst thing that can happen to a Husky.

Getting 15 excited dogs harnessed up to two sleds is no easy job. They were so anxious that I had to watch very carefully or they'd leave without me. And sure enough, the second we jumped aboard our sleds, we were skidding madly over the bumpy ice and away from camp. Now I know why there is no word for goodbye in the Inuit language. Who ever has time to say it? There was

the dogs some walrus meat as a special reward when we noticed a shape moving toward us. It was too small to be a polar bear, but too big to be a fox. We could hardly believe our eyes when we saw that it was Chipee.

Then, something terrible happened. He was about a stone's throw away when the ice began to break up under him. Before he knew it, he had skidded straight into the freezing water.

We couldn't lose a moment. Chipee had to be pulled out before he lost too much body heat. Tying one end of a rope around his waist and throwing me the other, George crawled across the treacherous ice. Just in time, he dragged Chipee out by the neck.

scarcely time for me to look back to see what poor Chipee was doing. But when I did, I could see that he was watching us.

At the end of four days our hunt had taken us about 120 miles (200 km) and our sleds were laden with walrus and seal. We were just giving

Chipee was lucky, for the water hadn't yet soaked through his thick, oily fur. And after shaking himself for a few minutes and running round and round, he was ready for his first meal in four days. Later, when we started to harness the dogs, Chipee quickly slipped into his position on the team, as if nothing unusual happened. But something had happened: Chipee had changed.

He didn't snarl at the other dogs. He didn't struggle when the harness was slipped over his shoulders. He didn't even fuss when George later stopped the sleds and tied canvas boots on the dogs to protect them from ice splinters. We crossed our fingers and, sure enough, Chipee continued to behave himself. Four days alone on the ice must have been a terrible ordeal for Chipee, and it seemed that he wasn't ever going to risk being left behind again.

RUFF JOKES

Q. What's the best way to keep dogs off the streets?
A. Put them in barking lots.

Q. Why did the dog jump into the river?
A. It wanted to chase catfish.

Q. What kind of dog says meow?
A. A police dog in disguise.

Q. What did the dog say the flea?
A. Don't bug me.

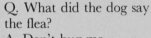

Q. What kinds of dogs do scientists have?
A. Laboratory Retrievers.

Q. What do you get if you cross a chicken with a dog?
A. A chicken that lays pooched eggs.

Q. What's taller sitting down than standing up?
A. A dog.

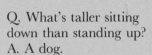

Q. Why did the dog go to court?
A. Because it got a barking ticket.

Q. What did one flea say to the other flea when they came out of the movies?
A. Shall we walk home or take a dog?

Q. How do you keep a dog from smelling?
A. Hold its nose.

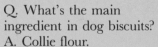

Q. What's the main ingredient in dog biscuits?
A. Collie flour.

SAY CHEESE

**These five pointers will make your dog
the star of your home pictures.**

Have a friend or family member help you take pictures. He or she can position the dog or command it to do tricks while you snap away.

Don't take a picture of a short dog in a garden of tall flowers unless, of course, you want to call your photograph "Spot the Dog."

Get on your dog's level. These eye-to-eye pictures are more fun than pictures of the top of your dog's head.

Take photographs of your dog against a plain background, but be careful that the background is a different color than your dog.

Put small, frisky dogs or pups that won't sit still on a low table. But make sure to have a friend stand by to catch any dog that jumps.

THINGS TO DO ON "DOG" DAYS

Here are some ideas for playing with your canine best friend.

Jog with your dog. But if you're near a busy street, put a leash on the dog.

Next time your dog feels happy and is wildly wagging its tail, count the number of wags per minute. Then see how many times you can wave your arm back and forth in one minute. How did you do?

How keen is your dog's sense of smell? Find out by wrapping a stone, a tennis ball, your dog's favorite toy and a tiny piece of meat separately in paper. How long does it take your dog to find the package with the meat in it?

Watch your dog the next time it's sleeping. Do its eyes flicker back and forth under its eyelids? That's REM, or rapid eye movement, sleep — a stage of sleep when people and animals including dogs, (scientists believe) dream. In fact, your dog's legs may "run" and its tail thump or swish as if it's chasing something or playing. It may even "talk" in its sleep. But you'll have to wait until your dog wakes up to ask it what it dreamed about.

Test your dog's tracking ability with this game. Leave your scent on a ball by rubbing it in your hands. After you let your dog sniff the ball, hide it in some bushes, but don't let your dog see where.

Trample on the ground to leave a scent trail. When you get back to your dog, tell it to seek. Get your dog started by pointing it in the right direction.

Some dogs love music and may even bark along with the melody. Play some records for your dog and see which music it likes the best. In fact, if you have to leave your dog alone in the house, it's a good idea to turn the radio on so it won't feel lonely.

TO THE VETS

Taking your best friend to the vet
may seem like a rough trip, but it's a
very good idea. The visit should take
place at least once a year—and it's
a great opportunity for you to get
answers to any questions you might have.

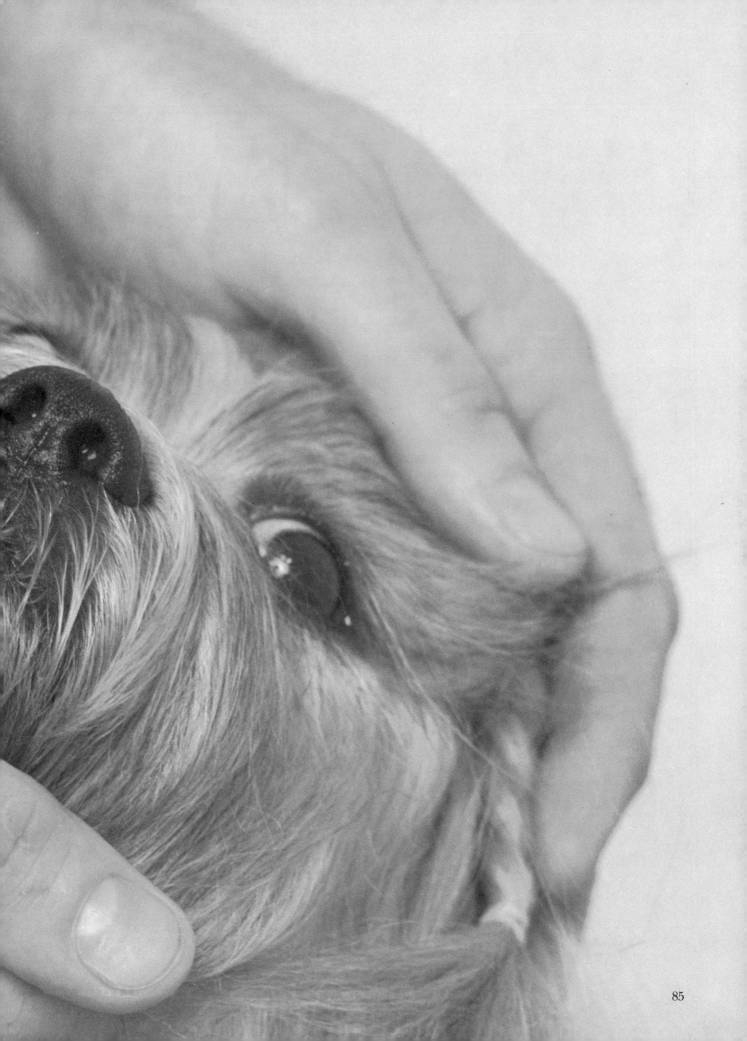

What should your vet check for? When the vet listens to your pet's heartbeat with a stethoscope he is making sure the beat is regular.

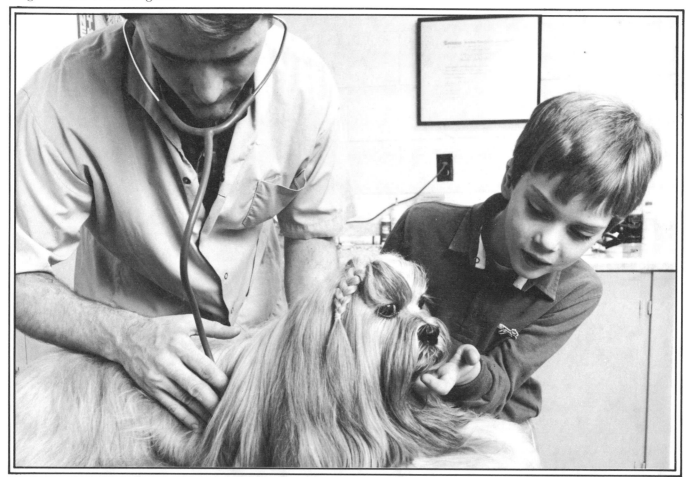

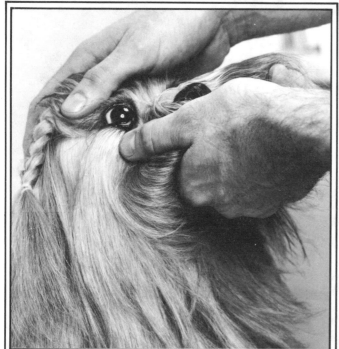

As with all creatures, your dog's eyes should be clear and bright. It's a sign of good health.

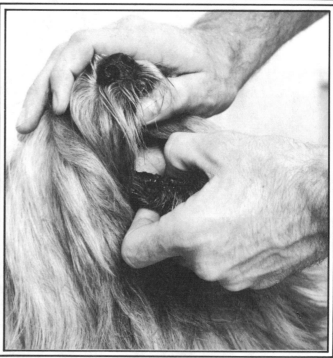

Teeth and gums should be healthy. To help keep them that way, give your dog chewy toys or dry dog food. Brushing teeth is also important—but check how to do this with your vet—never use people toothpaste.

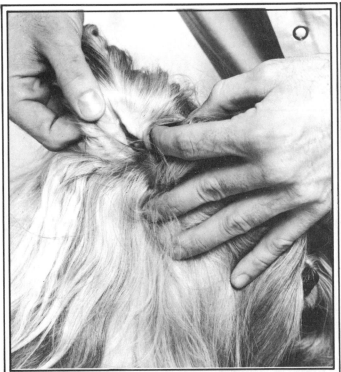

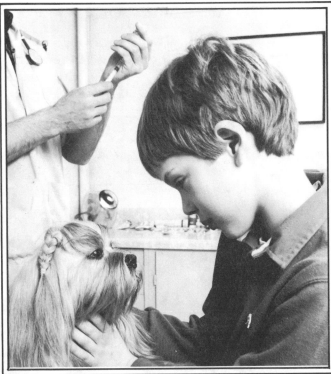

Are your dog's ears and skin healthy and free of infections or parasites? If not, the vet can help correct these problems.

Shots! Who likes them! Vaccinations every year will help your dog stay as healthy as possible. It's worth a moment of pain.

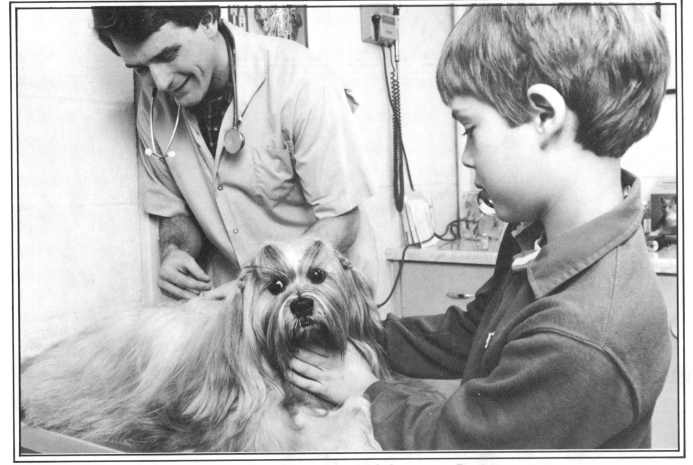

Always take a stool specimen to the vet's so the vet can check for worms. Dogs can get heartworms from mosquitoes, so you'll need to pick up medicine to prevent this. All is well. A healthy dog—hurray!

PUTTING ON THE RITZ

These dogs were seen at a summertime dress-up dog show. If they could talk, what do you think they would be saying?

A GUIDE TO DOG SHOW LINGO

Apron: the long hair on the throat and brisket forming a frill.

Barrelled: a dog with a very round chest.

Butterfly Nose: a nose with mottled skin.

Button Ears: ears that fold over in front, neatly drooping their tips forward.

Frog Face: a face in which the nose is extended and the jaw recedes.

Fly Ears: semi-erect ears in which the tips are not necessarily carried symmetrically.

Hare Feet: long, narrow feet with well-separated toes.

Kissing Spots: the attractive spots on the cheeks of some toy dogs.

Trousers: the hair on the hindquarters of a dog.

Feathering: the long fringes of hair as seen on the backs of the legs of setters.

Squirrel Tail: a tail that curves forward over the back, even at the root.

Tulip Ears: ears that are erect, slightly open and leaning forward.

BLUE RIBBON POINTERS

The first recorded dog show was held in England in 1859 with a total of 50 dogs competing. Today it's not unusual for more than 500 dogs to be in the same show. Though the rules and regulations of dog shows vary from country to country, the aim is the same: to pick the best dog of all. However, instead of being judged against each other, dogs are judged against an ideal standard set out for each breed. But before you rush out and enter your dog in a show, here's a look at some dos and don'ts.

PROFESSOR B. HOUND
PRESENTS
HIS
DOGGONE DIFFICULT
DETECTIVE
GAME

It's not as easy as you may think being a dog, and this detective game will show you why. Below are seven owners and their dogs. Can you spot the owners who are treating their dogs correctly and those who are not?

A helpful hint: you'll have no trouble with this game if you put yourself in my paws and see life from a dog's point of view.

Answers on page 96

Good dog

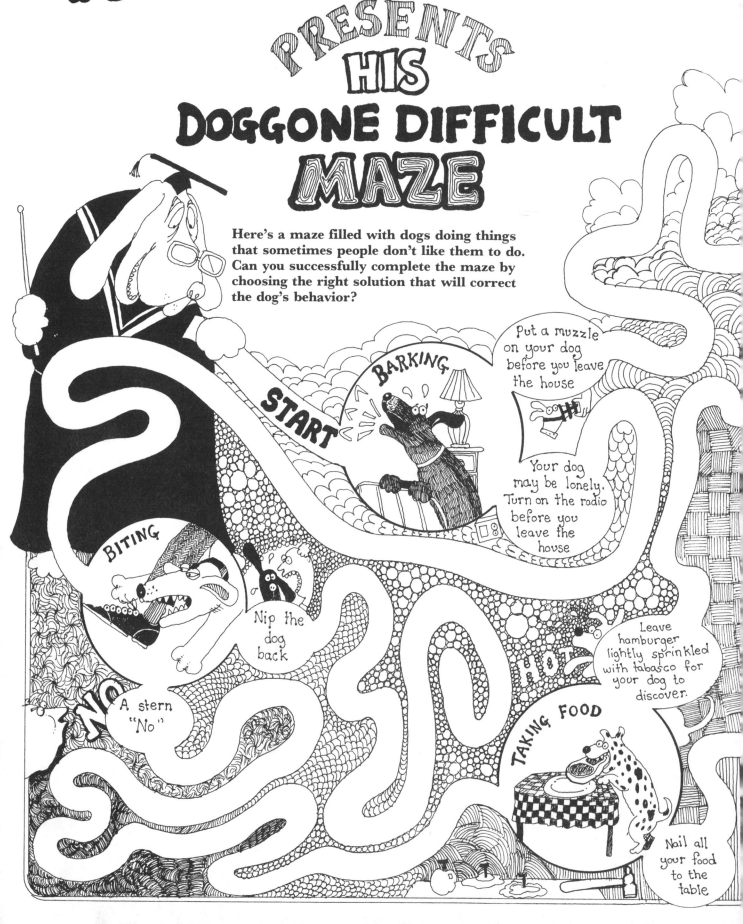

Answer to A DOG WHATSIT on page 51

The mystery dog has the body and head of a Bouvier des Flandres, the ears of a Welsh Corgi, the snout of a standard Schnauzer, the front legs of a Chow Chow, the back legs of an Irish Setter and the tail of a Poodle.

Answers to Doggone Detective Puzzle on pages 92-93

The following behavior should put any owner in the dog house:

1. It's best to let sleeping dogs lie and not wake them up by sneaking up on them and shaking them. This could startle a dog and make it cross. Imagine how you'd feel if someone woke you up with a vigorous shake.

2. Reward your dog for good behavior with praise and love—not food, especially junk food. You'll end up with a very fat dog.

3. There's no need to shout at a dog. Its hearing is much better than yours, so talk in a normal voice.

4. There's no point in scolding a dog hours after it has done something wrong. It will have no idea what's going on. Scolding is only effective if you catch your dog in the middle of doing something wrong or immediately after.

5. When you are training your dog, make sure that it can see what you're doing. Remember that it's much shorter than you, so get down to its level whenever possible. Loose clothing and baggy pants that flop around and block the dog's view shouldn't be worn.

This behavior is not only acceptable but it's something to wag a tail about:

1. Love is an important ingredient in training. The owner who is giving his dog a hug for good behavior is giving his dog extra confidence.

2. The owner who is training his dog to sit down wants to make sure that the dog understands the command. So the owner is demonstrating how he wants the dog to sit.

Credits

1, 2/3, 6/7, Stuart Sherwood; 10/11, 12 Yvonne Van Wyck; 13 Normunds Berzins; 14/15 Miller Services (Terrier, Basset, Daschunds & Spaniels); Normunds Berzins (Pekingnese & Springer Spaniels); 16 Normunds Berzins; 17 Tina Holdcroft; 18/19 Elaine Macpherson; 20/21 Stuart Sherwood; 22/23 Normunds Berzins; 24/25 Tina Holdcroft; 26/27 Elaine Macpherson; 28/29 Miller Services, Stuart Sherwood; 30/31 Elaine Macpherson; 32 Tina Holdcroft; 33, 34, Miller Services (Old English Sheepdog), Normunds Berzins (Scottie, Pug, Australian Shepherd, Chow, Afghan); 35/36 Miller Services; 37 Tina Holdcroft; 38/39, 40/41 Mark Thurman; 42/43 Anker Odum; 44/45, 46/47, 48/49 Tina Holdcroft; 50 Anker Odum; 51 Tina Holdcroft; 52 Wallace Edwards, 53, 54/55 Olena Kassian; 56/57 Wendy Lindsay, Lina Corbett; 58/59 Courtesy CTV Network; 60/61, 62/63 Lynda Cooper; 64/65 Maritta Tapanainen; 66/67, 68/69 Tina Holdcroft; 70/71 John De Visser; 72/73 Tina Holdcroft; 74/75, 76/77 Tom McHugh. Wildlife Unlimited P.R.; 78/79, 80 Fred Bruemmer; 81, 82/83 Tina Holdcroft; 84/85, 86/87, 88/89 Tony Thomas; 90/91, 92/93, 94/95 Tina Holdcroft.

Consultants

Dr. Alan Secord, Arlene Reiss, Kevin Seymour.

Special thanks to Dr. James Hysen (p.84/85, 86/87) for his assistance and patience, the use of his surgery at the Amherst Veterinary Hospital, Scarborough. Also thanks to "Snuffy" ('Champion I'm Aslands, Mirror Image, apa.) and his owner for their assistance (Page 84/85 86/87).

A big thankyou to the overall consultant, Dr. Alan Secord and to Dr. Gary Landsberg for special editorial assitance.

Acknowledgements:

Design Director: Nick Milton. A special thanks to Edith Davis, Sylvia Funston, Natalie Provenzano, Lyn Thomas, Val Wyatt.